JAZZ FAN LOOKS BACK

Other Books by Jayne Cortez

Pisstained Stairs and the Monkey Man's Wares

Festivals & Funerals

Scarifications

Mouth on Paper

Merveilleux Coup De Foudre: Poetry of Jayne Cortez and Ted Joans

Firespitter

Coagulations: New and Selected Poems

Poetic Magnetic

Fragments: Poetry of Jayne Cortez and the Sculpture of Melvin Edwards

Somewhere in Advance of Nowhere

Limited Edition

Intolerance (for the World Conference against Racism, Durban 2001)

Recordings (with music)

Celebrations and Solitudes

Unsubmissive Blues

There It Is

Maintain Control

Everywhere Drums

Cheerful & Optimistic

Taking the Blues Back Home

Find Your Own Voice

JAZZ FAN LOOKS BACK

By Jayne Cortez

Hanging Loose Press,
Brooklyn, NY

www.hangingloosepress.com

Printed in the United States of America
10 9 8 7 6 5 4 3 2

Hanging Loose Press thanks the Literature Program of New York State Council on the Arts for a grant in support of the publication of this book.

Cover art by Melvin Edwards
Cover design by Pam Flint

Acknowlegdments: Some of the poems in this book first appeared in *Sulfur* magazine.

Library of Congress Cataloging-in-Publication Data

Cortez, Jayne.
    Jazz fan looks back / Jayne Cortez.
        p. cm.
    ISBN 1-931236-10-0 (cloth) -- ISBN 1-931236-09-7 (pbk.)
    I. Jazz --Poetry. 2. Jazz musicians--Poetry. I. Title.

PS3553.O72J39 2002
811'.54--dc21   2001051989

Produced at The Print Center, Inc. 225 Varick St., New York, NY 10014, a non-profit facility for literary and arts-related publications. (212) 206-8465

TABLE OF CONTENTS

NOTES

As a young girl, I saw drummer Chano Pozo with the Dizzy Gillespie big band in Los Angeles, California, at Wrigley Field, 1948. When a new Charlie Parker record came out, I had it before most people in my neighborhood. I took piano lessons and harmony, played bass in the orchestra in junior high, and hung out at the record shop after school. I knew who Fats Navarro was when he was alive. I was a serious Jazz fanatic. I met Charlie Parker, heard Billie Holiday and Clifford Brown in person, and had a conversation with Duke Ellington. In fact, I met or heard most of the musicians mentioned in this collection, with the exceptions of Ma Rainey and Bessie Smith.

A portion of *Jazz Fan Looks Back* was produced in a special limited edition of two hundred copies in February 2000. It contains poems published and unpublished from 1968 to 2000. It is my poetic response to African and African American music, Blues, Jazz, Black Music, The Music and its environment.

I should like to thank Melvin Edwards, Denardo Coleman, and Christopher Winks for their help and contribution to the preparation of the manuscript. This book is dedicated to the memory of my mother, Ada Johns, who introduced me to music, and to my friend Bob Rogers, who supported my interest in culture.

TAPPING

(For Baby Laurence and Other Tap Dancers)

When i pat this floor
     with my tap

when i slide on air
     and fill this horn intimate with
the rhythm of my two drums

     when i cross   kick
scissor   locomotive

     take four for nothing
four we're gone

when the solidarity of my yoruba turns
joins these vibrato feet
     in a Johnny Hodges lick
a chorus of insistent Charlie Parker riffs

     when i stretch out for a chromatic split
together with my double X
     converging in a quartet of circles

when i dance my spine in a slouch
     slur my lyrics with a heel slide
arch these insteps in free time

     when i drop my knees
when i fold my hands
     when i decorate this atmosphere
with a Lester Young leap and
     enclose my hip-like snake repetitions
in a chanting proverb
     of the freeze

i'm gonna spotlite my boogie
     in a Coltrane yelp

echo my push in a Coleman Hawkins whine

i'm gonna frog my hunch in a Duke Ellington strut

quarter-stroke my rattle
      like an Albert Ayler cry

i'm gonna accent my march in a Satchmo pitch

      triple my grind in a Ma Rainey blues

i'm gonna steal no steps

      i'm gonna pay my dues

i'm gonna 1 2 3

      and let the people in the apple
go hmmmp hmmmp hmmmp

BRIGHT BROWN SUMMER

Lord Nelson
Star dusted on
Santa Barbara
in Max's free-town

>You and Lord
>preacher Brown
>stroking prayer bells
>as you ate the horn up
>you did

Moist fleshy lips
weeping willows
under a blue moon
on a new day

>Kissing the foot of
>Oh Woo Wee Doo
>smacking Blackies
>heart in a
>flashy mass spittle
>of fire
>stompin pride
>from muted cries
>on the truth hunt

Some of us heard
the delivered word—Clifford

>Keeper of the horn
>Young sputtering deacon
>in the spiritual choir
>singing with Fats & Freddy

Untouched by bets
and other Chets

even full-fledged taps
wouldn't begin to cut
the tone-blown love
flung from
the mack-mans bad tongue

How long has this Evening trach been Gone?
Gershwin How long has this been Going on?

HOW LONG HAS TRANE BEEN GONE (1968)

Tell me about the good things
you clappin & laughin

Will you remember
or will you forget

Forget about the good things
like Blues & Jazz being Black
Yeah Black Music
all about you

And the musicians that
write & play about you
a Black brother groanin
a Black sister moanin
& beautiful Black children
ragged...underfed laughin
not knowin —

Will you remember their names
or do they have no names
no lives — only products
to be used when you wanna
dance fuck & cry

You takin — they givin
You livin — they
creating starving dying
trying to make a better tomorrow
Giving you & your children a history
But what do you care about
history — Black History
and John Coltrane

No
All you wanna do
is pat your foot
sip a drink & pretend

13

with your head bobbin up & down

What do you care about acoustics
bad microphones or out-of-tune pianos
& noise
You the club owners & disc jockeys
made a deal didn't you
a deal about Black Music
& you really don't give
a shit long as you take

      There was a time
when certain radio stations played all Black Music
from Charlie Parker to Johnny Ace
on show after show
but what happened
I'll tell you what happened
they divided Black Music
doubled the money
& left us split again
is what happened

John Coltrane's dead & some
of you
have yet to hear him play
How long how long has that Trane been gone

and how many more Tranes will go
before you understand your life
John Coltrane who had the whole of
life wrapped up in B flat
John Coltrane like Malcolm
True image of Black Masculinity

Now tell me about the good things
I'm telling you about
John Coltrane

A name that should ring
throughout the projects mothers

Mothers with sons
who need John Coltrane
Need the warm arm of his music
like words from a Father
words of Comfort
words of Africa
words of Welcome
How long how long has that Trane been gone

John palpitating love notes
in a lost-found nation
within a nation
His music resounding discovery
signed Always
John Coltrane

Rip those dead white people off
your walls Black People
Black people whose walls
should be a hall
A Black Hall of Fame
so our children will know
will know & be proud
Proud to say I'm from Parker City — Coltrane City — Ornette City
Pharaoh City living on Holiday Street next to
James Brown Park in the State of Malcolm

How long
how long
will it take for you to understand
that Trane's been gone
riding in a portable radio
next to your son who's lonely
Who walks walks walks into nothing
no city no state no home no nothing
how long
How long
have Black People been gone

THE ROAD

Blue Stone in Memphis

Stony blue cries

in honky-tonk taverns

    on the road

    from K town

    to K town

      the road

the same road that downed

Bessie in the ground

and amputated round — way over in London Town

Where another Hank moans

Stony Lonesome

Bessie's arm was torn

when the Blues came down mean

Them Lowdown Dirty Blues

    Dancing Round

    Whining in Bessie

"Get Back Blues"

THEODORE

Heading for
the Lowlands
down 52nd street
Heard tell of
a fat man
who would make us
pray at his feet

His name was
T. Navarro
but they called him
Fats for short

They say
he had a scream
so mean
it make a
dead man cream
with a hum
from the slum
to make a
numb sister
come

He was
T. Navarro
they called him
Fats for short
Said
he wailed through
the Wailing Wall
Bounced with Bud
beyond Infidels
to let Ice
Freeze Red and
Moved it on out with Max
to clean E.C.'s Guilt

and shout

"You must remember this
I lived
and played my horn
the best that I
knew how
and all I got
those who said
they dug the music cats
was:
        "You should do this
        You shouldn't do that
        cause I'd do thus and so
        if I was you Fats."

Let me tell you one thing
he didn't need nothin
to make him play that way
but he took a whole lot
of something
        to keep them
        bats & flies away

Fats
no longer fat in size
Gone from XXL
        to ssz

        Died inside that
        not-so-shy
        but lonely Hag
        friend of the devils
        known as Mrs. Scag

Yes remember
the name was
T. Navarro
they called him

Fats for short
and his life
was snuffed by
inadequate people
whose minds were
dry as chicken-shit-slime

3 DAY NEW YORK BLUES

It's tuesday night
in ole possum face new york city   sweet daddy
        spit upon sadness
in this fist of three vines of two dark lips of
sunken blisters in my need more   need more
need more lovin sometimes baby please please please

And already it's wednesday mornin
in the deep end of my river
and like a woman
locked outdoors in a storm
        i got those mean wet kill me kill me
        stroke me baby do me tonight blues

May i present thursday
in moonshine of my weepin willow
in the lonesome road of my groanin
moanin   sanctified   dignified   sweet smellin
hoochicoo

Comes friday
and this life beggin request
dead and gone
in noon time of my frisky whiskey money bag
cuttin mood

Juice up new york   juice up

        Cause i got a fine warm satisfyin
screamin deep sea divin good feelin papa
hoppin skippin jumpin flyin
back home to me

OPENING ACT

To be the opening act
and absorb all slobber
all praises
all stares
all insults in a rhythm tube of
fallopian teeth

To be the opening act
and not forget the odor of cockroaches
in a diamond miner's eyeball
flame of a dead flint
listen to this suspect number one
because to be the opening act
and plant feet in asses of corrupt politicians
without a time clock without correct wages
without profits without bitterness
without a breeding place for pain
is a bitch
so pass the word around

To be the opening act
and know when to duck when to salute
when to cover up
when to fight
when to scream when to dive into your solitude
and detoxify whistles in your kidneys
salt dry curses in your eardrums
and then laugh into the drunken gallbladders of the night
you have to be rich in blood vessels to
bury that act in someone's mouth at 3 o'clock every morning
so don't fuck with me
I want to be the opening act between this planet and the sun
in health   in sickness   in death
I said primp on your own time baby
because I'm walking the entire motion of space
in rawflesh of this opening act to end all acts

and I don't have to impose myself on anybody
so throw your wig into the ocean
I know I'm the opening act of acts here
because all of a sudden
someone blew smoke in my face and yelled booooo

SOLO FINGER SOLO

When evening goes down into its jelly jelly jelly
into drainpipe cuts and stitches and vaccinations
protruding from arms

And spirit of the five-by-five man pushes
his sweet potatoes in the air
feather daddy leaps into a falcon of tropical bird squats
rubber legs swing into off-beat onijos   onijos
then into your solo finger solo
the blues chantress jumps up and
repeats her nasal volcanic chant calling

Count Basie Count Basie Count Basie

And Count Basie
you burn through this timbale of goose flesh rhythms
a drop of iodine on your starfish lips
the intonation of your kiss of melodica trilling
into a labyrinth of one o'clock jumps
into corpuscle flashes of the blues torpedo
the erupting volcano of the blues shouters chanting your name

Count Basie   Count Basie   take 'em to Chicago   Count Basie

And Count Basie
you punctuate this strong bourbon mist of gamma globulin breath
a mixture of chords like serpentariums coiling
from the deep everglades of your body
and when the luscious screams of three-headed root doctors split
Kansas City reeds in unison with this triple tapping
double stopping slow grinding loosey butt night swinging
with the blues chantress
erupting volcano of the blues torpedoes chanting your name

Count Basie
you reach through the bottom of the music
way down between cross rhythm vamps
below air stream of the lowest octave

into depths of a sacred drum
and Count Basie   Count Basie   Count Basie
how powerful and dignified and exquisite and direct and
sharp
your solo finger solo is

ROSE SOLITUDE

(For Duke Ellington)

I am essence of Rose Solitude
my cheeks are laced with cognac
my hips sealed with five satin nails
i carry dreams and romance of new fools and old flames
between the musk of fat
and the side pocket of my mink tongue

Listen to champagne bubble from this solo

Essence of Rose Solitude
veteran from texas   tiger from chicago   that's me
i cover the shrine of Duke
who like Satchmo   like Nat (King) Cole
will never die because love they say
never dies

I tell you from stair steps of these navy blue nights
these metallic snakes
these flashing fish skins
and the melodious cry of Shango
surrounded by sorrow
by purple velvet tears
by cockhounds limping from crosses
from turtle-skinned shoes
from diamond-shaped skulls and canes
made from dead gazelles
wearing a face of wilting potato plants
of grey and black scissors
of BB shots and fifty red boils
yes the whole world loved him

I tell you from suspenders of two-timing dog odors
from inca-frosted lips
nonchalant legs
i tell you from howling chant of sister Erzulie

and the exaggerated hearts of a hundred pretty women
they loved him
this world sliding from a single flower
into a caravan of heads made into ten thousand flowers

Ask me
Essence of Rose Solitude
chickadee from arkansas that's me
i sleep on cotton bones
cotton tails
and mellow myself in empty ballrooms
i'm no fly by night
look at my resume
i walk through the eyes of staring lizards
i throw my neck back to floorshow on bumping goatskins
in front of my stage fright
i cover the hands of Duke who like Satchmo
like Nat (King) Cole will never die
because love they say
never dies

IF THE DRUM IS A WOMAN

why are you pounding your drum into an insane babble
why are you pistol-whipping your drum at dawn
why are you shooting through the head of your drum
and making a drum tragedy of drums
if the drum is a woman
don't abuse your drum   don't abuse your drum
                              don't abuse your drum
I know the night is full of displaced persons
I see skins striped with flames
I know the ugly dispositions of underpaid clerks
they constantly menstruate through the eyes
I know bitterness embedded in flesh
the itching alone can drive you crazy
I know that this is America
and chickens are coming home to roost
on the MX missile
But if the drum is a woman
why are you choking your drum
why are you raping your drum
why are you saying disrespectful things
to your mother drum your sister drum
your wife drum and your infant daughter drum
if the drum is a woman
then understand your drum
your drum is not docile
your drum is not invisible
your drum is not inferior to you
your drum is a woman
so don't reject your drum
don't try to dominate your drum
don't become weak and cold and desert your drum
don't be forced into the position as an oppressor of drums
and make a drum tragedy of drums
if the drum is a woman
don't abuse your drum   don't abuse your drum
                              don't abuse your drum

INTO THIS TIME

(For Charles Mingus)

Into this time
of steel feathers blowing from hearts
into this turquoise flame time in the mouth
into this sonic boom time in the conch
into this musty stone-fly time sinking into
the melancholy buttocks of dawn
sinking into lacerated whelps
into gun holsters
into breast bones
into a manganese field of uranium nozzles
into a nuclear tube full of drunk rodents
into the massive vein of one interval
into one moment's hair plucked down into
the timeless droning fixed into
long pauses
fixed into a lash of ninety-eight minutes screeching into
the internal heat of an ice ball melting time into
a configuration of commas on strike
into a work force armed with a calendar of green wings
into a collection of nerves
into magnetic mucus
into tongueless shrines
into water pus of a silver volcano
into the black granite face of Morelos
into the pigeon-toed dance of Mingus
into a refuge of air bubbles
into a cylinder of snake whistles
into clusters of slow spiders
into spade fish skulls
into rosin-coated shadows of women wrapped in live
iguanas
into coins into crosses into St. Martin de Porres
into the pain of this place changing pitches beneath
fingers swelling into

28

night shouts
into day trembles
into month of precious blood flowing into
this fiesta of sadness year
into this city of eternal spring
into this solo
on the road of young bulls
on the street of lost children
on the avenue of dead warriors
on the frisky horse tail fuzz zooming
into ears of every madman
stomping into every new composition
everyday of the blues
penetrating into this time

This time of loose strings in low tones
pulling boulders of Olmec heads into the sun
into tight wires uncoiling from body of a stripteaser on the table
into half-tones wailing between snap and click
of two castanets smoking into
scales jumping from tips of sacrificial flints
into frogs yodeling across grieving cults
yodeling up into word-stuffed smell of flamingo stew
into wind-packed fuel of howling dog throats slit into
this January flare of aluminum dust falling into
laminated stomach of a bass violin rubbed into red ashes
rubbed into the time sequence of
this time of salmonella leaking from eyeballs of a pope
into this lavender vomit time in the chest into
this wallowing time weed of invisible wakes on cassettes into
this off-beat time syncopation in a leopard skin suit
into this radiated protrusion of time in the desert into
this frozen-cheek time of dead infants in the cellar
into this time flying with the rotten bottoms of used tuxedos
into this purple   brown   grey gold minus zero time trilling into
a limestone-crusted Yucatan belching
into fifty-six medallions shaking
into armadillo drums thumping

into tambourines of fetishes rattling
into an oil slick of poverty symbols flapping
into flat-footed shuffle of two birds advancing
into back spine of luminous impulses tumbling
into metronomes of colossal lips ticking
into double zigzag of calluses splitting
into foam of electric snow flashing into this time
of steel feathers blowing from hearts
into this turquoise flame time in the mouth into
this sonic boom time in the conch
into this musty stone-fly time sinking into
the melancholy buttocks of dawn

COBRA CLUB

To dance the razor-drill dance in the cobra club
suck off the rain crows' holler
pull into a fantail paper-lip-smacking-reefer straight out
at midnight

for you on double elbows in a butane truck

I have the crazy bones laughing in alligator stomps
I have the railroad tracks you call my thighs
flat-talking like sepia trumpets
I hold the scorpion and tequila in my mouth
we embrace the paranoid sea
the tip of a stinging kilimanjaro licked

Let it dry like fly specks between cyclones
in this lobe burnt pepper day
in the dizzy spells falling head
in belly bush navels with sesame crabs

There will be other chicken wings at the window
other leaves turning back into mosquito drums
other legends in dark stockings rolled down
you will tangle in the long rope solitude menses
of solitary fungus
you will eat buckshots off the evening
and wear them like flea bites in new cities
we will blow through this gravel pit shadow of poverty together
like a rada of black rum flowing with the depths
of this cobra club funk
an alkalized cadenza of stale metallic tongues pushed back

I SEE CHANO POZO

A very fine conga of sweat
a very fine stomp of the right foot
a very fine platform of sticks
a very fine tube of frictional groans
a very fine can of belligerent growls
a very fine hoop of cubano yells
very fine   very fine

Is there anyone finer today   olé okay
Oye   I say
I see Chano Pozo
Chano Pozo from Havana Cuba
                              You're the one
You're the one who made Atamo into
a tattooed motivator of revolutionary spirits

You're the one who made Mpebi into
an activated slasher of lies

You're the one who made Donno into
an armpit of inflammable explosives

You're the one who made Obonu into
a circle of signifying snakes

You're the one who made Atumpan's head strike against
the head of a bird   everynight everyday
in your crisscrossing chant
in your cross river mouth
                              You're the one

Oye   I say
Chano
what made you roar like a big brazos flood
what made you yodel like a migrating frog
what made you shake like atomic heat
what made you jell into a ritual pose
Chano Chano Chano

what made your technology of thumps so new so mean
I say
is there anyone meaner than Chano Pozo
                              from Havana Cuba

Oye
I'm in the presence of ancestor
                              Chano Pozo
Chano connector of two worlds
You go and celebrate again with
the compañeros in Santiago
        and tell us about it
You go to the spirit house of Antonio Maceo
and tell us about it
You go to Angola
and tell us about it
You go to Calabar
and tell us about it
You go see the slave castles
you go see the massacres
you go see the afflictions
you go see the battlefields
you go see the warriors
you go as a healer
you go conjurate
you go mediate
you go to the cemetery of drums
return and tell us about it

Lucumí Abakwa Lucumí Abakwa

Olé okay
Is there anyone finer today
Oye I say
did you hear
Mpintintoa smoking in the palm of his hands
did you hear
Ilya Ilu booming through the cup of his clap

did you hear
Ntenga sanding on the rim of his rasp
did you hear
Siky Akkua stuttering like a goat-sucking hawk
did you hear
Batá crying in nago tongue
did you hear
Fontomfrom speaking through the skull of a dog
did you hear it   did you hear it   did you hear it

A very fine tree stump of drones
a very fine shuffle of shrines
a very fine turn of the head
a very fine tissue of skin
a very fine smack of the lips
a very fine pulse
a very fine encuentro
very fine   very fine   very fine
Is there anyone finer than
Chano Pozo from Havana Cuba
Oye I say
I see Chano Pozo

YOU KNOW

(for the people who speak the you know language)

You know
      i sure would like to write a blues
you know
      a nice long blues
you know
      a good feeling piece to my writing hand
you know
      my hand that can bring two pieces of life
      together in your ear
you know
      one drop of blues turning a paper clip
      into three wings and a bone into a revolt
you know
      a blues passing up the stereotype symbols
you know
      go into the dark meat of a crocodile
      and pinpoint the process
you know
      into a solo a hundred times
      like the first line of Aretha Franklin
you know
      like Big Mama Thornton
you know
      i sure would like to write a blues
you know
      if i could write me a blues
you know
      a blues that you could feel at the same time
      on the same level like a Joe Louis punch
you know
      a punch that could break a computer
      into an event like Guinea Bissau like Namibia
you know
      if i could write me a blues

you know
    a nice long blues
you know
    an up to the minute blues
you know
    a smack dab in the middle of depression blues
you know
    a blues without incidental music
you know
    without spending time being incidental
you know
    if i could write a blues
you know
    a blues without the popular use of the word love
you know
    without running love love   love in   the ground
you know
    a serious blues
you know
    a significant blues
you know
    an unsubmissive blues
you know
    a just because we exist blues
you know
    a blues
you know
    a terrible blues about the terrible terrible need
    i have to write the blues
you know
    if i could write a nice long blues
you know
    a nice long blues
you know
    it sure would feel good to my writing hand
you know
    you know
you know

DRYING SPIT BLUES

Tonight the whooping moan of invading blues
    with its clef of troubled hearts
with its double stomp burn of woman flesh
    spitting with the whirlwind of spitting cobras
spitting with the meaning of Anna Nzinga
    flash flooding blues
of great blues migrations
    the great blues of howling Sudan
great blues in a conflict of Nubian throbs
    among the faces chiseled from Memphis
among the cataracts spitting from Ethiopia
    the great blues of drying spit
with its escalator of razors
    forefinger of pistol whips
quadrangle of knuckle bones
    basin of fish hooks
equator salt
    the whooping taste of invading blues
of broken whistles
    radiated foxholes
a grenade of camel hair
    calypso of neck scars
old blues
    intravenous blues
blues with a procession of blows
    the blows in mouth of the goatheads of death
a commemoration to famine
    right up to our chests
after skulls of invading blues
    of bombed-out groans
150 rockets between screams
    meat hooks smelling into smells of needle-tracked ribs
dead crows fried feathers spoiled calamares
    and eyes of sculpted slugs
and silver ants on lower lids painted charcoal

and long teeth in amber gels
      and tongue flaming tongue of sweetheart rings
of ruby snakes with veins of iridescent smoke studs
      a squadron of lips made of cockleburrs
      a salty dirge of sapless pinchers
a mirage of pulsing green roosters
secret dogs
polychrome spirits
      head-quart of bullface throat slitters
right up to our chins
      sparkling without lizard juice
mutilations without mucus
      a concave of widowfish entering flies
a circle of jackals cocked on the moon
      a cylinder sun without holes
and once again warships rush to other ports
and once again relief is too late
and once again a shriveling solution
      the code name for buzzards
wrist-bones on altar of another jaw
      illuminations
right up to our nostrils
in howling Sudan
      in Nubian throbs
in faces chiseled from Memphis
      the shrinking shrines of whooping flesh
of invading skeletons
      of spreading Saharas
of drying spit
      tonight's Blues

ATELOGO

I am hitting the drum three times
        in memory of
red wine   feijoada   & Marietta
        in memory of
cassava   cachaca   & Marietta
        in memory of
books   boxes   & Marietta
        in memory of
conversations   translations   & Marietta
        atelogo   atelogo   atelogo

HELEN

When they talk about singers
they never talk
about Helen Humes
who could
gut the bucket
how high the moon it
& hey babareebop it to ya

NO SIMPLE EXPLANATIONS

(To the Memory of Larry Neal)

There are no simple explanations
not for the excesses
not for the accumulations
not for the lips of magnetic lava
not for the liver of explosive slits
not for the heart
       ready to shoot off like a volcano
There are no simple explanations

The altar will not fit another skull
and there are no more volunteers
no mixture of eyelashes and drops of blood
                  in the circle
no alliances drinking together
              in a night of dead events
no bulletproof faces in the air
no mask of erosion fermenting in slobber
no fetish trunk of sacrifices in disguise

Only the space of exasperation left by the advance
only juice from heat of its possession
the injunction of shadows
collectivity of ants
tongue of deified soot
flesh of incarcerated bones
but no simple explanations

Not for madness
reproducing itself through the uterus in the throat
not for sharks
having feeding frenzies in the middle of foreheads
not for
sentimental passwords of vomit splattering pages
No simple explanations

Let the index finger
        take responsibility
                for its smell
let the chickens protrude from drums
let the lagoon   the boat   the ancestors
        enter pores of a poet of pretty smiles

This piece is passing up the motif of sorrow
                let it pass
let the words split and erupt and dry
          into snake pulsations
Spit three times
      into ruby dust of your own snot
and paste it
      on callus of your self-conscious itch

I say lung   fire of mouthpiece tremble
still warm and metal stone
conjuration and syntax
inverted stump under solitary root
          of erratic falcons
weed of pain   of rupture   of panic
let it go down
     like body and soul
        in the horn of Coleman Hawkins
Sink into the insurrection of red shanks
into the high-pitched voltage of mosquito hums
into liquefied ankh of Egyptian flames
sparrow house bubble of quiver
let your divination fall
     like body and soul
        in the horn of Coleman Hawkins

Ritual fart
and navel and rebellious stink
urination and energetic repulsion
poetic orgasm and guttural belch of erotic storm
let your dynamism grunt
I say

42

make it shake forward like shimmering tumors of okra stew
shake forward on a speckled canvas of menstrual bandages
shake into sucking tubes of midnight flies
into the sub-dominant tilt of flinching eyeballs
into the intrinsic elasticity of violent impulses
Conform to evolution of your own syllables
to revolution of your own stanzas
because
suddenly it will be too soon
suddenly it will be too late
suddenly it will be too sudden
and there'll be no tuning forks left
in palm of a poet on a cold morning
no deposits of fat left
on neck of a blues at the crossroads
no spell of inspiration waiting
at foot of a cocaine pyramid
no juju leaves hidden
in the center of the whirlwind

Only abusive forces in absolute opposition to revolts
only burial grounds of radioactive mud
only bellies of unfinished poems
and time dismantling itself between invisible sticks
but no simple explanations

Not for the flesh of incarcerated bones
not for the tongue of deified soot
not for the womb of "hoodoo hollerin' bebop ghosts"

No simple explanations

CHOCOLATE
(CHOK-OH-LAH-TAY)

Hey Chocolate
they say in your high-blooded fingers
full of fetish dolls
hurricanes run

And on those fuchsia-dotted lips
where African ballads drink
solitude intensifies

And with your teeth down deep in these overtones
you form a snake each night that spits

And I hear a spell shaking
Vera Cruz almost bending
flying crying aye aye aye

aye Chocolate
they say in your mouthpiece
full of baby talk and conga beats
superstitious flames cut through sentimental
rainbows full of love affairs intruding
and formless realities sloping
weaving overlapping half-moaning
you blow your axe aye aye aye

Chocolate
they say through your open horn full of dancers
laughter comes
and in your purple velvet mute
you keep a walk so fine
a rumba so strong
your yuka in root
a green smell   a low pitch
a shrilling vibrating cry
stridulating through the swamps through the city
through the time effects

you keep the mambos inflamed
you keep the sambas in tune
you keep a tango in slides aye aye aye Chocolate

They say
into your breath full of wa-wahs women scream
and with your knees dipping deep into these spirits
you carve your shout
and I hear the signals barking
blood vessels almost breaking libating on the sands of Havana crossing
fast blades falling hot brass melting
tongue forks tuning holding spreading leaping
squawking rhythms rising modulating salsas striking
aye ya ya ya ya ya yo Chocolate
lyrical Chocolate Choc-o-late Chocolate
I like the way you play your horn
through the bell through the navel through the impulses who
through the sweat through the veins through the felt-covered boom
you keep the tangos in oil
you keep the merengues in chrome
you keep a cha-cha implunged aye aye aye aye Chocolate

They say in your cheeks full of staccato
a witch doctor lives
and between your orange-striped gums
where circles rotate
secret ancestors knock

And I hear you grinding spinning
parading through the crowd like a hawk flaming
smoking
you blow your axe aye aye aye
aye Chocolate I like the way you blow your horn man

RIBS & JAZZ FEST 94

Barbecue smoke
Corn on the cob
Piggly wiggly piggin out on pig
Nice venue
This chewing and licking of fingers in my face
Hooray
The monitors are up
The music is happening
& I'm very optimistic

DRUMS EVERYWHERE DRUMS

Drums everywhere drums
drum that remain
to booster thighs in its radar
in its thump of a bass without
being beggar
sunlight   midnight having to be barfly
having to be bullfrog
having to be drums
                    drums
burnt drums to clear the skin among dreams
flint of antibiotic dawns
potash and cinnamon   sperms rising
with an algebra of swamp drums
no longer pyrex teeth
topaz excrement
angular nightmares
no longer ax-shaped lips
pierced corten buttocks
at the bottom of fermented mud drums

Drums flowing with a mask of zircon tornadoes
pickup band holding spirals of whiplash
in its bric-a-brac in its eyefold of mashed tendons
rimless springs
entrances funneled with catafalques of
embroidered signal drums

Drums made from rivers
made from a multiplication of dance steps
made from catfish heads in a tongue's embrace
made from a rosette of orange rosin cradle cap
with impulse spotted like seclusion and
revolution decorating its drum
with memory grease made from Nat Turner's body
drums preoccupied in cheeks of ancestors
twirling into footprints into snare drums into ceremonies

into shoe shine rags
the dust on those skins on those reeds
arranging armatures of black feeling
into street octaves of liberation drums of
membranes close to the sun's memoirs
and life duct of this brillo atmosphere
drums the size of flea bites drums that are fly heads
cork and plantain drums vase oil drums and
flannel flame wreaths of iridescent toenail drums
Everywhere drums

Drums
brushing whiskers of imagination
into ink ripples of compelling pompadours
drums grinding into steel
silver wires out of nostril bells
embalmed with images inoculating drums into feet spikes
of new canoes and new patterns
of new hurricanes
drumming with red palms of passion
drumming with massacred villages in Mozambique
drumming with uncombed look of a message
moving through heartbeats of six female drums
everywhere drums

Drums of acrobatic wombs
of bladders and trumpets engulfed
in a drum of opening elbows
the alto wind of sapling drums
fluorescent drums of benzine marshes
barracuda drums
in asphalt drum of nipple star drums of hunger drums
indexed between ovums
between floral ligaments
and the rhythm of rickets
drumming in a hollow of blues
baritone callus on rainbow covenant
of pickled heart drums

breast wheel of drums
fished up through pores of pimento
through ovations of bloated gills
babbling goiter drums holding
fissures of thumps in a coil of favelas
drums
the frequencies in position
drums
the sulphurated humidity of brooding rolls
broken pistons and cockpits of drums
remaining with pabulum
with fluorine
with city whistles and forks entering drums
of borax and wild hairs
turbo-jetted throat drums
chrome-studded fangs of stomping stampedes
into tom-tom diaphragms
of black diamond pearl drums
everywhere drums
peninsula of my berserkness drum
axle of my hydraulic cough drum
diatonic drums
crazybone of my hyenaic laughter drum
thrill of a triad of electrode drums
everywhere drums

Drums in rufescent blades of Roxbury wind
tall cool fine drums
cry drums scream drums
dream interpretation of jungle spells and
tenement fire drums
searching through the buckeye drums
reaching for washboards of African blood drums
laughing drums emerging drums
precisions of blackness drums
drums whispering drums climbing
drums migrating into pedals and moods
of finger-popping tambourine drums

brick drums   crawfish drums
drums of new belches   drums with old mercurochrome
undulating armpit drums
cubano drums
sparrow leg strokes of tongue-tied drums
opal pool cues
ground nut pyramids
hey peewee from Panama drums
sanukadei   sanukadei
and my wide mouth paradiddles of adupe adupe drums

And these bragging drums of sparkling cans
and these home-brew tear-jerking drums
and this bong bong deep in the cowbell of Zimbabwe
and staccato beating drums
crossing the Limpopo
crossing death-drums foreskin drumming against drums
Fierce drums
growling drums
echo drums
over mojo whoop whooping drums
out of coo coo ka hooka drums
ear drums   khaki drums
drums made of dynamite
drums made from elephant yelps
Fulani drums   Fon drums   Ga drums
drums of new juniflips
drums of ancient mardi gras
Asantehene drums Senufo drums
and my indigo lip-smacking conga drums
tightening
drum rhythms
into mush-mouth rhythms child-birth rhythms
Ibo god house rhythms
melancholy bellies crossed in a knife of rhythms of
rhythms
from baba's calabashes of rattling rhythm drums of
drums to drums of brass cymbals of drums

dazzling with hummingbirds
with guava skins   with cowrie shells
with jellyfish   with kola nuts
with cobalt and uranium and
Mandingos on the road to kokomo drums
everywhere drums
spit drums from Oduduwa drums
everywhere drums
domo domo domo domo domo domo drums
Oduwa drums everywhere drums   everywhere drums
Ekuse

GRINDING VIBRATO

Blues woman
with the beaded face
painted lips
and hair smeared
in the oil of Texas

You were looking good and sounding beautiful
until the horseman wanted your thunder
until the boa constrictor wanted your body
until syringes of upright hyenas
barbwired your meat to their teeth and
pushed behind your ears
inside your mouth
between your vagina
scabs the size of quarters
scabs the size of pennies
the size of the shape of you
all pigeon holes and spider legs colonized woman
funky piece of blood flint
with blue graffitied arms
a throat of dead bees
and swollen fingers that dig into a swamp of broken
purrtongue

Blues woman
who was looking good and sounding beautiful
with those nasal love songs
those strident battle-cry songs
that copper maroon rattle resonator
shaking from your feet to your eyes
the sound of water drum songs
grinding vibrato songs to work by to make love by
to remember you by
Blues song woman who was looking good and sounding
beautiful
until you gave away your thunder

until you gave up your spirit
until you barbwired your meat to teeth
and became the odor of hyenas
uprooted woman with the embalmed face
pall bearer lips
and hair matted in the mud of Texas
how many ounces of revolution do you need
to fill the holes in your body
or
is it too late to get back your lightning
is it too late to reconstruct your blues song sister tell me
is it too late for the mother tongue in your womanself to
insurrect

JAZZ FAN LOOKS BACK

I crisscrossed with Monk
Wailed with Bud
Counted every star with Stitt
Sang "Don't Blame Me" with Sarah
Wore a flower like Billie
Screamed in the range of Dinah
& scatted "How High the Moon" with Ella Fitzgerald
as she blew roof off the Shrine Auditorium
                            Jazz at the Philharmonic

I cut my hair into a permanent tam
Made my feet rebellious metronomes
Embedded record needles in paint on paper
Talked bopology talk
Laughed in high-pitched saxophone phrases
Became keeper of every Bird riff
every Lester lick
as Hawk melodicized my ear of infatuated tongues
& Blakey drummed militant messages in
soul of my applauding teeth
& Ray hit bass notes to the last love seat in my bones
I moved in triple time with Max
Grooved high with Diz
Perdidoed with Pettiford
Flew home with Hamp
Shuffled in Dexter's Deck
Squatty-rooed with Peterson
Dreamed a "52nd Street Theme" with Fats
& scatted "Lady Be Good" with Ella Fitzgerald
as she blew roof off the Shrine Auditorium
                            Jazz at the Philharmonic

ABOUT FLYIN' HOME

What would you say to yourself
if you had to lay on your back
hold up the horn
& play 99 choruses of
a tune called Flyin' Home
exactly as you recorded it
55 years ago
& what would you think
if you woke up in the afternoon
& your head was still spinning with
voices shouting
Flyin' Home blow Flyin' Home
& what would you do
if someone whispered in your ear
hug me kiss me anything
but please don't play Flyin' Home
& what if a customer said:
tonight I'm having sex with
a person who has been up
in a flying saucer
so please funk me down good with Flyin' Home
& what would you think
if someone started singing
Yankee Doodle Dandy
in the middle of your solo on Flyin' Home
& what if you had to enter
all the contaminated areas in the world
just to perform your infectious version of
Flyin' Home
& what if you saw yourself
looking like a madman
with a smashed horn
walking backward on a subway platform
after 50 years of blowing Flyin' Home
& what would you think to yourself
if you had to play Flyin' Home

when you didn't have
a home to fly to
& what if Flyin' Home became
your boogie-woogie social security check
your oldie-but-goodie way out of retirement
& was more valuable than you
I mean somewhere
in advance of nowhere
you are in here
after being out there
Flyin' Home

SAMBA IS POWER

In Brazil
I sambaed on the road to João Pessoa
I sambaed on the beach of transparent crabs
I sambaed to sounds of iron bells
in State of Bahia
I sambaed while eating muqueca
while watching capoeira
while wearing Oxum belt made by
maker of ritual objects in Salvador
I sambaed through São Paulo Airport
I sambaed onto dark-skin   light-skin   African
Indian   Portuguese situations of struggle
I sambaed into translations while drinking batidas
with writers at Eboni Bookstore
I sambaed while waiting for a short mustached
so-called mulatto who swore
he was a Yoruba Babalawo   I sambaed
I sambaed onto corner of handcuffed
Afro-Brazilian men
sambaed next to women who were
spinning pulsating & assaulting police cars
I sambaed into house of candomblé
into congress of Black culture
into Perfil of African Literature
I sambaed
I sambaed next to the red buildings of Exu
I sambaed with Gege & Egbas
I sambaed into trance of Yemaya
I sambaed with Oko
I sambaed in front of the daughters of Santos
I sambaed against walls of political graffiti
I sambaed with Xango
I sambaed with Mae do Samba
My samba wrapped in orixa ribbons
my samba mixed with human smells & feijoada
my samba infused with vatapá and caipirinhas
the uphill samba bursting out of my feet

the samba whistles hollering out of my navel
the samba fetishes buzzing high
in samba dome of my soul
as I sambaed & sambaed & sambaed & sambaed
I sambaed diagonally through Recife floods
sambaed upward through steel cages of Brasilia
sambaed away from alcohol fumes
in Copacabana
sambaed behind homeless children
with soccer ball eyes
sambaed past dealers dealing drugs
sambaed into costume room
in Comunidade Mangueira
sambaed in front of Protestant missionaries
who preached that samba is sin
but samba is life
samba is friction
samba is power
& I sambaed & sambaed & sambaed
sambaed into circles with Rei Momo
as he shook his heavy flesh in slow motion
sambaed next to young women quivering
their brown calves in quadruple time
my samba getting drunk off the high speed rhythms
my samba embedded with bass drums of cachaça
my samba parading & scorching teeth of
the Rio de Janeiro sun
my samba absorbing the forest stench
of poet from Amazonas
my samba squatting down & wiggling up
as I sambaed the samba of my memory
the samba of my fantasy
the samba of my samba
because samba is life
samba is friction
samba is power
samba is everything
that's why I sambaed & sambaed & sambaed

TALK TO ME

(For Don Cherry)

Like the sound	of the rain
Boiling up	in the sky
Beat it down	to the ground
Bring it in	with the wind
Plant your tone	through the zone
Move on back	smear your axe
With the stream	where you dream
Send those notes	over here
do it now	speak on out

SOLO

Fill your horn	with the clouds
Turn around	pass on through
Like the sun	& the stars
Possess the road	exile the code
Maintain the flow	metaphor the space
Pepper the night	pulsate the grove
Like the rain	like the snow
Throw it down	talk to me

I GOT THE BLUE-OOZE 93

I got the blue-ooze
I got the fishing in raw sewage blue-ooze
I got the toxic waste dump in my backyard blue-ooze
I got the contaminated drinking water blue-ooze
I got the man-made famine blue-ooze
I got the dead house dead earth blue-ooze
I got the blue-ooze
I got the living in a drainpipe blue-ooze
I got the sleeping in a cardboard box
                         waiting for democracy to hit blue-ooze
I got the five hundred year black hostage
                         colonialism never stops blue–ooze
I got the francophone   anglophone   germanophone
                         lusophone   telephone   blue-ooze
I got this terminology is not my terminology
                         these low standards are not my standards
                         this religion is not my religion and
                         that justice has no justice for me blue-ooze
I got the blue-ooze
I got the gang banging police brutality blue-ooze
I got the domestic abuse battered body blue-ooze
I got the ethnic conflict blue-ooze
I got the misinformation media penetration blue-ooze
I got the television collective life is no life to live
                         and this world is really becoming
                         a fucked-up crowded place to be blue-ooze
                  I got to find a way out this blue-ooze
                  because the blue-ooze
                  will make you sorry
                  that you ever had
                  the blue-oo-oo-ooze
                  I got the blue-ooze
                  I got the blue-oo-oo-ooze

SONNY'S CARNIVAL

Sonny swinging in
like great heavyweight champion he is
that fierce hunter with every initiation
encrusted in belly of his axe

low to high tone endings smoking like
a charcoal forest
melodic variations on cowboy tunes disappearing into
Mohawk ghost markings under Manhattan bridges to Brooklyn

& what a cluster of phonetics
transcribing through saxophone lecturing to trumpet in
teacher/student consultation
at Beacon Theater with Wynton
on Sonny's night
of Sonny's island

& even in corniness of his quotations
"Jeannie with the light brown hair"
the music is clear & pure & Sonny

HOWLING

(For Allen Ginsberg)

Allen couldn't sing the Blues
So he started howling
Not like Howlin' Wolf but
Howlin' Allen
Howling all over the place
About sex & God & global excess of carbon emissions
Howling about soil erosion
Plutonium
The proliferation of firearms
& runaway nuclear reactors
Howlin' Allen
Howling like a threatened endangered mammal
Howling that inborn instinctive howl
That introspective retrospective collective howl
That blunt unbending howl against war
Against corporate leaders and political corruptness
A mean in-your-face howl
An agitated howl against co-opted colleagues
Allen howling with the declining whales
Howling a long intense rampaging howl
A meditative in-depth soulful joyful liberated hypnotic howl
A drunk sober howling complex of seductive tongues,
Heated finger fetishes, intoxicated manifestoes
exotic erotic encounters
A howling existential beatnik collage of poetic massages
Allen couldn't sing the Blues
So he became Howl

A MILES DAVIS TRUMPET

There are the ivory trumpets from Africa
the silver trumpets found in drawings
on walls of Egyptian tombs
telescoping trumpets from China
trumpets that live in Tibet
Spanish-speaking trumpets of Spain
& then
there is
that trumpet
with solitary feeling of sound
splashing through rough woodshed of Charlie Parker
splashing the sound of distance
                        in trumpet
                        against orchestra
trumpet circling within box
                    of a box
                of controlled settings
        trumpet
patinaed with layers of rust & spit
grooving inside the groove surface
trumpet
with bell of funk fired up
in middle extremities
between bass & treble
thunder & whistle
Unmuzzled cheeks of brass
inflated storm of mutes
elastic electric Elegba
that trumpet

There are the oceanic shell trumpets
buzzing Southern Indian trumpets
natural Arabian trumpets
fast-talking Cuban trumpets
European-inspired valve trumpets
trumpets with great ears

& husky tones & avant-garde ways
trumpets   fanfaring   dirging   parading
& giving military salutes

There are
side-blown trumpets
side-winder trumpets
straight trumpets
sweet trumpets
Satchmo trumpets
Oliver trumpets
Bolden trumpets
Little Jazz trumpets
Red trumpets
Rex trumpets
Dorham trumpets
curved trumpets
Dizzy trumpets
Clark trumpets
Hot Lips trumpets
Fats trumpets
pocket trumpets
Cootie trumpets
Farmer trumpets
Brownie trumpets
Cherry trumpets
& then there is
that short dark popping trumpet
covered in a mask of
New York hipness & fame
that trumpet
with another hairdo
another change of aspirations
another half-nelson in
a constellation of dust
another motif in
        terrycloth turban
another hoarse voice of

Orin to ti Orunwa
that trumpet

That trumpet
with the sound of chance
the sound of prediction
the sound of invention
the sound of migration & madness
& fluidity of solitude
& mathematical flurries
& blasted bridges
& dynamism within
collectivity of the hunt
that trumpet
with jom
with spirit
with secret sound systems hidden
behind sunglass fetishes
that trumpet
has a throat
which sits outside
of its body
sits on top of the wind
on top of the band
with explosive pucks
mystical rain spittle
aboriginal tongue toot toots
that trumpet
that trumpet is
the militant   mellow   melodic   magical
miraculous   minimalist   Miles Davis trumpet
that trumpet

SO WHAT

So what
if I spend
the rest of my life
living on invisible mouth
of an imaginary saxophone
        breathing in
        & blowing out
        polluted air
        in August
doobee doobee doobee suck suck
all the way through this tunnel
      so what
      if you sniff
the monumental torture smell of power
            like
toe jam piss & rotten cabbage
on sleeves of my last overcoat
        don't jump off
        throw up
        fall down
I want you
to touch my hair like
        so many flies
understand these boogers I eat
        Don't worry
        it's the business of death
        to be hungry
I only sit
in its lap
like a buzzard
one lick at a time
        doobee doobee doobee suck suck

MUSIC FLYING

Music flying   tacos flying
Banners flying   & you want to fly too
I love it
In my cerveza negra modelo tasting mood
In my huachinango smell of fishkills
Imagine
Someone has invited
This very green place to lunch
In my red sauce
They have made me Veracruzana
Of the stuffed iguanas and
I am swallowing a rainstorm of Afro-Spanish tongues
while hiccuping like a firecracker
popity popity pop pop pop

ENDANGERED SPECIES LIST BLUES

A snow leopard does not know
it's on the endangered species list
Mr. & Mrs. Crab are not into
destroying the world
they are crawling to the mud flats
to take in some rotten insects
It's not what's up that's going down when
you smell yourself on
the threshold of extinction
It's you and your portable chemical toilet
going to hell under friendly fire
It's you and your missile receptor
exploding to pieces

It's not what's up that's going down

The person who OK's biological weapons
should not cry about the stench of
new diseases
The one who cuts off the trees
so the orangutans can't hang
should not wonder about ecological devastation

It's not what's up that's going down
It's what's down that's going up

It's not what's up that's going down
It's what's down that's going up

BUMBLEBEE, YOU SAW BIG MAMA

You saw Big Mama Thornton
in her cocktail dresses
& cut off boots
& in her cowboy hat
& man's suit
as she drummed &
hollered out
the happy hour of her negritude
                              Bumblebee

You saw Big Mama
trance dancing her chant
into cut body of
a running rooster
scream shouting her talk
into flaming path of
a solar eclipse
cry laughing her eyes into
circumcision red sunsets
                              at midnight
                              Bumblebee

You saw Big Mama
bouncing straight up like a Masai
then falling back spinning her
salty bone drying kisser of music
into a Texas hop for you to
lap up her sweat
                              Bumblebee

You saw Big Mama
moaning between ritual saxes
& carrying the black water of Alabama blood
through burnt weeds & rainy ditches
to reach the waxy surface of your spectrum
                              Bumblebee

69

You didn't have to wonder
why Big Mama sounded
so expressively free
so aggressively great
once you climbed
into valley roar
of her vocal spleen
& tasted sweet grapes
in cool desert
of her twilight
                    Bumblebee

You saw Big Mama
glowing like
a full charcoal moon
riding down
Chocolate Bayou Road
& making her entrance
into rock-city-bar lounge
& swallowing that
show-me-no-love supermarket exit sign
in her club ebony gut
you saw her
get tamped on by the hell hounds
& you knew when she was happy
you knew when she was agitated
you knew what would make her thirsty
you knew why Big Mama
heated up the blues for Big Mama
to have the blues with you
                    after you stung her
                    & she chewed off your stinger
                        Bumblebee
              You saw Big Mama

MAINTAIN CONTROL

Where are you going   Where have you been
Where are you going   Where have you been

When you rush to the job
& time clock the card
then step up production
to pay for corruption
but have no deductions
to pay for your pension
pay for your pay cut
pay for your strike fund
to Maintain Control   Maintain Control   Maintain Control

Where are you going   Where have you been
Where are you going   Where have you been

When you throw down your coat
& kick off your shoes
& drink down your booze
& turn on the beat
& strike up a groove
to wear out your feet
& wear out the drummer
trying to wonder
what is that number to Maintain Control
Maintain Control   Maintain Control

Where are you going   Where have you been
Where are you going   Where have you been

When you eat up the eats
& drink up the drinks
& smoke up the smokes
& crack up the crack
& blot out your visions
& blot out your values
but find no solution

to your pollution
to Maintain Control   Maintain Control   Maintain Control

Where are you going   Where have you been
Where are you going   Where have you been

When you numb down your brain
& dilate your eyes
& coke up your nose
& asbestos your sniff
& procaine your lips
& jolt up your heart
to stagnate your life
     & push out your violence
use up your body
     & push out your violence
count up your gadgets
     & push out your violence
lock up your face
     & push out your violence
litter up the planet
     & push out your violence
push out your violence   push out your violence

To Maintain Control?   Maintain Control?   Maintain Control?

Where are you going   Where have you been
Where are you going   Where have you been

& what have you done
& who made you do it
& what did you see
& who made you see it
& what do you need
to pull up your courage
& what do you need
& how will you get it
to maintain control
of who's in control

to maintain control
of what's in control
to maintain control
Maintain Control   Maintain Control   Maintain Control

MR. LOUIE

Oh Mr. Louie
how did you get the right
to gut bucket the Blues
& go strutting with some barbecue
up the lazy river
yeah you hoodoo boys
always changing word pitches &
getting haunted when
it's summertime down south
Oh Mr. Louie
you had your fill
seventy years of the 20th century
seventy years and you thought
you'd leave us a little taste of
that talking trumpet from Storyville
Oh Mr. Louie
how did you put that
tip of the rocket tone in your horn
yeah you hoodoo boys always rambling
& breaking new ground in the dialogue
always laughing   looking possessed &
leaving handkerchiefs of sweat on the bandstand
you hoodoo boys always snapping fingers &
getting a glow on when
you take back music
from the lazy river
Oh Mr. Louie
blow a tune for me

MUSICAL EMPLOYMENT

To talk about resentment
You have to talk about domination
And if you talk about domination
You have to talk about standards
And if you talk about standards
You have to talk about the reality of camouflage
And if you talk about the reality of camouflage
You have to talk about entertainment
And if you talk about entertainment
You have to talk about dress codes
And to talk about dress codes
You have to talk about bandstand manners
And if you want to talk about bandstand manners
You have to talk about the club that banned Bird
And to talk about the club that banned Bird
You have to talk about finance without romance
And romance without finance

PHOTO OP BLUES

Africa was already Africa
way before men danced around
in shirts made of mirrors & feathers
& before a man in a three-piece pinstriped suit
with leopard claws around his neck
started dreaming of being
a Hollywood Chaka Zulu
but instead became
the chocolate Zulu candy bar known as "Gotcha"
Africa was already Africa
way before Jonas Savimbi
donned his uniform made of diamond studs
& plastic landmine fragments &
sat with an American president
for a photo op which he demanded as
part of his payoff for keeping his army
in the business of maiming people in Angola
Africa was already Africa
before the Prince arrived wearing
a red checkered tablecloth on his head while
worming his way into another womb after
viewing the Slavehouse on Gorée Island
and way before Leopold put on his military czarist outfit
and came down the chimney
to destroy the Congo
& make another fashion statement on
the fashion plate of oppression
Africa was already Africa

STRIKE UP THE BAND

At midnight
in your rusty industrial cockpit
                of oxtail stew
in your hiccuping buttocks made
                radioactively ready to prance
khaki uterus &
                AK-47 tongue
blow through your ghost words
your coyote microphone
your wildebeest virtuoso crying pipe
let chickens get tired of chicken shit
your throat is like a two-headed drum
your nostrils like a honkin saxaphone mojo tool
the dog is howling
the door is slamming
the path is moving like a local donkey toward
the canceled dance concert
the banned cockfight
& the cocoa leaves are so vocal
so cadaverish
so patinafied
so wide-eyed owlish
let the termites nest in
                your electric bass heart
let the song of self-interest fall down on
its knees in a rockability vagina grunt
let the reefer-seeded moon squat in
                horse breath of a young wino
let dawn babble through a mouth of mildew blankets
there is nothing better than wearing
your own shoes
your own panty liner
your own jock strap
your own sweat
inside your own navel of archaeological digs
                heat up the site
whoever possesses the land will possess your bones &
                makde love to your night life   uh hunh
strike up the band

THE REVOLUTIONARY ORCHESTRA

I used to sleep
in houses made of
flattened steel drum barrels
and wake up between
bulldozer blades
they labeled me
Queen of Impermanence
until I stomped on Apartheid
in the Grand Apartheid Ballroom
with Jacob Morenga &
Revolutionary Orchestra of Namibia playing Free Jazz
We knew how to darken airs of superiority
Sink the fascist system in its frenzy
& celebrate victory
in consolidated mines while
drinking rio tinto zinc wine
& dancing dances called
Subversive Entertainment Act 3
and Bullet Hole of Censorship Finished

THE GUITARS I USED TO KNOW

Guitars
with excavated rhythms
with maps & bridges
& the sweetness of sugar from
                              Pernambuco
                    from Nacogdoches
              from Itta Bena
from Chitunguiza
Guitars
with names like
          Edolia Adelia
                    Freddie Mae Johnny Boy
Matakenya Machado
          Zodwa and Letty Bea
Guitars
Guitars full of
inlaid shark fins
apocalyptic bloodstained finger boards
intoxicated paradoxinated coils
indigenous fusionous realms
collisional digital switches
reverse reverb shrills on flatbed trucks
          Guitars
The guitars trembling into
ultrasonic tempos into
insurrectional gestures into
scrunching wild-dog yowls
Yowling
with the mother-of-pearl habit
of living in isolation
with the plastic tradition
of being too sociable
with the inflammatory projections
hyperventilating into
trances stances romances guitars
The guitars I used to know

Guitars
arriving from Chicago
from Takoradi
from Casamance
from Texas
from Toledo
       & I can hear
       The guitars calling themselves Lightnin'
       I can hear the guitars calling themselves T-Bone
       I can hear the guitars calling themselves Minnie
       & I can hear the black lacquered guitars
       & the red guitars & the big brown rusty guitars
       & cadillac green guitars & majestic purple guitars
       & metallic blue Guitars
acoustically dipping down whispering
"Don't make me wait too long now"   Guitars
electronically screaming
"I heard you beating your lover last night"   Guitars
zigzagging through the crown & shouting
"I'm not losing my mind over you baby"   Guitars
marching around and yelling
"I'm gonna cut your power line"   Guitars
turning flips & whining
like ritual killers   Guitars
vamping on bandstands
& laughing like howler monkeys   Guitars
clearing paths
& humming like violins from Swaziland   Guitars
hollering half tone half step higher than
ordinary catastrophes   Guitars
circling with strings on teeth and crying ouch
Guitars
gigless   strapless
hanging upside down like
disembodied robots
between dilapidated flamenco boots
exhausted pubic bones

80

& torn alligator shoe tongues
Guitars
hanging upside down while
people imitate specialty of
the next machine Guitars hanging
upside down before resurrecting and exploding
straight out into the air
of numb thumbs
of snap slaps
of steel squeals
of moan zones
of pecked necks
of drill trills
of joke smoke
of set frets
of ride slides
of squeeze freeze
of plunk funk
of ping ting
of ting ting ting ting ting
Guitars
I'm talking about
The guitars I used to know

FINA LEONE

(for Leon Thomas)

We went into
process of your delivery
peeped your many Africanisms
deciphered your superstitions
and swallowed omens from your
yey yey yey yey yey yey yey yey
Mr. Eat Up The Blues In New York City
everybody knew you preserved &
created musical instruments in
your mouth of collective memory
                    Fina Leone
we heard enhancement of
your cultural identity elevated
as you invented a new way of singing &
multiplying metallic vibrations onto the
defensive front of your master plan
Mr. Yodel Throat In Botanical Study Of Leaves At Duke's Place
you made the turn around
brought back the ancestors
the dirges
the old field hollers
the squawking falsettos &
low turbulent vocaltudes through
didjeridoo of your drum kit cheeks
you cleared the way-ye
with your Bemba Mbamba Yoruba Pygmy
East St. Louis Kikongo Harlem compilation of tones
Mr. Let The Rain Fall From Me   Boom Boom Boom Boom

WHY NOT

(for Babs Gonzales)

Why not
let Babs
dominate
this night
with his
thirty-year
rite of
      oo bop she bam

Horns imitating him
as he imitated them
in up-tempo grooveness
      of Expubidence
a riffology collaboration
      a sha ba dah ba doot doot
      in front of
sheel-lee-ah doo bee dah
      rejection into
      an injection of
oo daba doo bay doo yey doo yey doo
      Itself
      a home
      demonstration
      of those
      flat sharp
      natural sensations
      swinging
      at the end of the wind
      of a big ole nasty
      tenor saxophone ya ya ya yawl lapowl
      and why not

Why not
let Babs
drop his

bitter stream dream elaborations
      his
gravelly back throat stroke of
           bold premonitions
      his
fermented chest rest nest of
unvomited insurrections
      into
bopology explanations
tongue-blistering configurations
confrontations quotations
      in celebration
      of those
      metal-tipped
      melodious drips
      in lips
      on fire
      after midnight
         and why not

      Why not
      let Babs
      leave
      his hot
      orikiisms
in bandstand blood of the blues
in amber lights of city tubes
oo ya cooing and oop pop a dahing
      on his way to
      ee ee ee doo blah blee
      blee blah doo ee ee ee ee
         and why not

LAST NIGHT

Last night
I dreamt about
subway trains
chartreuse books
& Aimé Césaire who
looked like John Lee Hooker
in a band with Sonny Stitt
at this niteclub in
Zengeza section of Chitunguiza where
chibuku drinkers were drinking
and women snuff sniffers were sniffing &
Olmec sculpture face of
fighter Joe Louis was shadow boxing between
musical notations of Ngare gare
see you later see you later

TAKING THE BLUES BACK HOME

I'm taking the blues back home
I'm taking the blues back to where
the blues stealers won't go

I'm taking the blues back home
because the blues stealers like to steal
when they think they have nothing of their own
I'm taking the blues back home
I'm taking the blues back to the fire of the spirits
I'm taking the blues back to the
damp undergrowth
I'm taking the blues back to where
the blues stealers won't go
I'm taking the blues back home

I'm taking the blues out of the mouth of the stealers
I'm taking the blues out of the western stream
I'm taking the blues back before somebody sings
"Ain't nobody's business if I steal your blues"
I'm taking the blues back home
I'm taking the blues back home
before Robert Johnson comes from
the graveyard to say
"The blues has been crapped on"
I'm taking the blues back to the crossroads
I'm taking the blues back to the bush
I'm taking the blues back to the place
where the blues stealers won't go
I'm taking the blues back home before
Langston Hughes returns to say

"They've taken my blues again and gone"
I'm taking the blues back home
I'm the owner of the blues
& I'm taking the blues back home
The blues that came to me from the slave dungeons
the blues that came to me from the death trails

the blues that came to me from my ancestors
the blues that came to me in a spell that tells me
through birth that I'm the owner of the blues
from a long time ago
I'm the owner of the blues from a long
long long long time ago
I'm the owner of the blues
& even if somebody says
they have a right to sing the blues
I'm still the owner of the secrets in the blues
from a long time ago
I'm the owner of the blues
& even if somebody pays to play & use the blues
I'm still the owner of the blues
from a long time ago
I'm the owner of the blues
& I'm taking the blues back home
I'm taking the blues back to where
the blues stealers won't go
I'm taking the blues back home
I'm taking the blues back home

TEARING UP THE CATHEDRAL

I didn't think the poem
was going anywhere
until it became zombified
& started moving on its own
started floating and leaving the paper
& staring straight ahead
started swallowing pencils
drinking ink
crowing like a rooster
& flying in the air
until it became zombified
& started sucking on salt
twanging like metal scrapers
tearing up the cathedral at
the Sacred Jazz concert
& falling backward
into a resting place for blizzards
I didn't think the poem was going anywhere

FIND YOUR OWN VOICE

Find your own voice & use it
use your own voice & find it

The sounds of drizzle
on dry leaves are not
like sounds of insults
between pedestrians

Those women laughing
in the window
do not sound like
air conditioners on the brink

The river turtle
does not breathe like
a slithering boa constrictor

The roar of a bull
is not like
the cackle of a hyena

The growl of a sea-leopard
is not like the teething cry
of a baby

The slash of a barracuda
is not like
the gulp of a leaping whale

The speech of a tiger shark
is not like
the bark of an eagle-fish

The scent of a gardenia
is not like the scent of a tangerine

Find your own voice & use it
use your own voice & find it

AFTER HOURS

I am not sucking on a form
to get drunk off of its content
I am not pre-booking space in
non-smoking section of the imperial pipeline to
sell used cars   pussy   & industrial waste
I get no thrill from smelling mildewed curtains
watching dead moth in paprika
or sitting all day in the
bow wow of french horns inhaling
graphite breeze of iodine mist in honor of
involuntary spasms
no one is chewing on my warm diaper of acid rain
& I have no kiss-ass explanation for the question
"what is Jazz"
I live the routine of my routine
& when the female porcupine chatters
when the blue-face mandrill drills
I write a poem
taking a look at myself looking
& it's very clear and under surveillance
time rotating its butt in my face
& dearly beloved
I have already been
violated by survivors of the flood
so do not sweep while I'm eating
do not cover my pot with your lid

SUNNY SIDE OF THE PAGE

Art comes out
when it comes out
It comes out
as invention
inventing itself
inside steeplechase of
embraceable perdidos
bongo beepin and peepin through
stareyes of melancholy leap frogs leaping
as imagination imagines itself
blowing deep vibratoless slurs through
encrusted mouthpiece whistling like
old flaming rocketships
roaring in from Kansas City
with messages made of
musical flyspecks on
sunny side of the page of
unknown titles at
borders of disorderly time
tico tico ticking
on tip of terrifying tocks
talking anthropology talking ornithology
the study of birds
and the study of humans eating birds
like this
like that
on the day Charlie Parker married the universe
and universe
became universally hip
to fact
that jazz is
the African heart transplant
which keeps on keeping
western music alive

Art comes out when it comes out

it comes out like a saxophone in
a porkpie hat
it comes out like a saxophone weeping on Chelsea Bridge
like a saxophone covered in bird feathers
it comes out in blood oath tune of Cherokee
in subversive unruly rhapsodies
fanfaring finger leads
tongue swiftness adrift on reeds
meticulous melodious coupes indeed
dripping with wax and koko shouts
booming with valve oil and tobacco spit
dancing its ghost-of-a-chance dance
its African heart-transplant dance
keeping western music alive
and changing directions
into funky stupendous
next century of
pollution & eyeballs
going off to
scrapple in the apple with Mohawk
Chi Chi   Marmaduke   & Billie
bouncing into
the everything you are is you
advancing in a great Chi Wara headdress

WHAT'S HAPPENING

What's happening
You'll know what's happening
when you see Pedro the poet
selling condoms and poetry books
and hear the man of god
choking on his sexual contradictions
you'll know what's happening
when you see computers going to sleep on
shoulders of their secretaries and
hear workers dismantling governments
you'll know what's happening

What's happening
An intellectual is marching around like
a great humanitarian but won't pay his
child support that's what's happening
And on the lower east side of New York City
a Doris Day look-alike is imitating the voice of
Louis Satchmo Armstrong while
the minister of unnecessary information
gets his hair curled
That's what's happening
The musicians are making facial expressions acting
like they're really playing something complex
                    and are not
That's what's happening
& me? Me?
I have already dropped a half inch of
slobber on a certain line
I have already placed parachutes on
two mountains of paper
OK. It's only one word in three hours
but look at you
look at you
Your job is to be a singing raisin
He's a dancing cornflake

You're a smiling commode
She's a walking roll of toilet tissue
He falls on the beach like
a sack of empty bullet shells
She's forced to sit like a ground-based
missile interceptor in the tourist area while
commander in chief invades Panama and
shoots Panamanians democratically to
enforce human rights and burn up another flag
That's what's happening
And there are other drug dealers butting
                    heads in the dark
other equal-opportunity killers on
                    the horizon
other fraudulent financiers manipulating money
                    and doing the hand jive
other corrupt hotel chain owners with
nice clothes and dirty drawers
That's what's happening
Meanwhile
the meter "maids" are still giving parking tickets
and the gospel singers are still taking clichés
                    and beating them to death
and the xmas tree crews are out discovering the
deepest hole of their consciousness in the donut shop
and little ladies in long coats are walking in
competition with big ladies in tight pants
and here we are between the emergency exit of
                    a closing bank
and the ambulance entrance of an aging nuclear reactor
waiting for the economic recovery of our dreams
and that's what's happening
that's what's happening

SOMEWHERE A WOMAN IS SINGING

Somewhere a woman is singing
five different scales at the same time for
every stingray boppin in Savoy Ballroom
she is singing Savoy   Savoy
this energy's coming from me Savoy   Savoy
I'm sinking my soul in you Savoy   Savoy
oh how my spirit dilates
how my silence pulsates
in between these faces in you   Savoy
Savoy Savoy Savoy

Somewhere a woman
superimposing her
supernatural nest of robins
inside nature of singing Savoy
instinctively takes possession of the moon
spins it forward from tune deck of incidental tunes
covers it
with her scatology spittle
rolls it to edge of her edge
and cuts up space like
the great space cutter she is
this woman
flying through porthole of her shipwreck
kicking in all the subversive signals
she had suppressed in self-examination booth
of ancestral tongues
this woman pushing back the romantic
overgrown mangrove of used songbooks
to step out with a saturday night coupe of riffs
everything lovely and sweet and lovely
in her retrospective mouth of
multiple time systems
mesmerizing and signifying to
all the stingrays boppin in the Savoy Ballroom
Savoy Savoy Savoy

PASTEL ROOM

Big Jay wanted me to
Strut around the club with him as
He blew "Harlem Nocturne"
He wanted me to holler "Blow Big Jay"
As he lay on the bar honking his horn in
New York City

But it is thirty years later
He is not the plump Cecil Jay McNeely in Watts
Or the walking tenor sax man looking for
Dancers dancing the Pachuco in Aliso Village
Or the kneeling guy blowing between legs of
Dancers dancing the Texas Hop in the Barrel House
Or the bebopper bopping Los Angeles bop in
Jam sessions at the Pastel Room

It is thirty years later on the rug of his bald spot
& all his sexy solos have been co-opted
Recycled & rocked
Clearly what he needs is not another horn
But another idea
& that idea is in him
So Blow Big Jay

MAKE IFA

Make Ifa make Ifa make Ifa Ifa Ifa

In sanctified chalk
of my silver painted soot
In crisscrossing whelps
of my black belching smoke
In brass masking bones
of my bass droning moans
In hub cap bellow
of my hammer tap blow
In steel stance screech
of my zumbified flames
In electrified mouth
of my citified fumes
In bellified groan
of my countrified pound
In compulsified conga
of my soca moko-jumbie
MAKE IFA MAKE IFA MAKE IFA IFA IFA
In eye popping punta
of my heat sucking sap
In cyclonic slobber
of my consultation pan
In snap jam combustion
of my banjonistic thumb
In sparkola flare
of my hoodooistic scream
In punched out ijuba
of my fire catching groove
In fungified funk
of my sambafied shakes
In amplified dents
of my petrified honks
In ping-ponging bomba
of my scarified gongs
MAKE IFA MAKE IFA MAKE IFA IFA IFA

I WAKE UP EARLY

I wake up early in the morning
sit and think about
divination trays
cow bells
oil drums
the sky all rusty with gongs
I jump up as
day snaps back through
maze of ashy Nubian thighs
poems entering my head
from left side of midnight
I put them on paper
touch down
in lower register of the turmoil
let one shape
tell the whole story
like a Thelonious Monk plunk
the motion
clear
distinct
rooted in what it is
what it was the
instant I hit it
the moment everything said click
unpredictable
imagination sticking out its tongue
unrepeatable
sound boards posing like
the sun that changes
into a bird standing
on crocodile teeth
transmissions
acquisitions

use it
go beyond it
just write and let it happen
          hangnail in afterbirth
          saltfish motif on steel

BETTY

The voice of May
Is the voice of Betty Carter
Betty the bandleader in control
Betty the mother of special melodies
Betty the young girl singer with Hamp and Ray
Betty pure Betty
Independent Betty
Betty the spring festival of Egyptian trombones
Deep Betty
The passionate humming bird in a bebop cap
Fresh Betty
The great wildflower of May

JOHNNY BLOWING & POINTING HIS MACHETE

Johnny
checking his watch and
clapping in time with
piano players' bouncing shoulders
Johnny
dancing with his saxophone
together they are foreshadowing paraphrasing and shadow boxing
they are fragile   frail   fast-fingering   fierce and flying
they have that walking-the-high-wire-without-net sound
that newborn-baby yelp
that swift-attacking shark-slashing whisper
that misty humidifying cloud-foaming hurricane hiss
that slow-motion moaning into deep up-tempo swinging which says
"You never been there before
so take the lights down MF
take the lights down MF
you never been there before"
Johnny
blowing & pointing his machete cutting saxophone
& together they are roaring through Blue Note Club like
two unapologetic bears
they are steaming through their confinement &
striking the stage with
whatever the possibilities of the music
and even the music knew
of no one more vulnerable
no one more expressive
than Johnny

HEMPHILL TONIGHT

Tonight
all the contradictions
all the interjections
all the agitations
all the languages spoken with eyebrow gestures
all the ecstatic shoutings
all the ironic notations
all the ideas proliferating through precious metallic spit
the profound scientific soundings in
rara mouth of irradiated teeth
the revelations mixed in gentrified space
the indigenous key snap calculations
the chronology of hats left in the doorway
the rising typhoon of sweat circling docks
the exclamatory pitches
the drunk investigative medicines flowing through
clavicles of the airshafts most
magical medicinal musical moment of awareness
the sky turning around in shipyard of the body
rage intensifying its
Texas Dogon A.D. Coon Bid'ness stint of
nomad flint on firefly wings
and already
one leg waiting for the other at the sound check

HOUSE OF RUBBER 92

Jazz Fan returns home to see
the East West Motel
smoking itself in mirror on the ceiling
the Kentucky Fried Chicken shack burning to
a crispy minstrel chalk
the one-hour cleaners cleaned out of existence
shopping malls mauled
jazzy Mai Tai Club knocked out
the auto body shop beyond repair
the bridal salon in a wedding dress made of old flames
the check-cashing concerns checking out
the cash machines drunk on molotov cocktails
the gym running on a treadmill of ashes
the Seoul Bar gutted
the beauty supply shop smoldering under
embers of hot curling irons
drugstores cooking in chemicals
hamburger joints electrocuted
the house of rubber tires fuming
& still standing with funeral parlors and churches
is a sign that says:
Los Angeles Proud Sponsor of Those Who Carry the Torch

CARTOONING WHENEVER THE MUSIC STARTS

Whenever the music starts
they start
Veronica, Betty, and Archie talking to their Jughead
as Little Orphan Annie amplifies her voice
to gossip with Ms. Snow Whiteman who
blows smoke signals in
the direction of Paul Bunyan who is walking in
after chopping down all the trees
and is now in the house breathing like
a buzz saw in competition with
bass player's solo as Uncle Ben brings in the rice and
Nancy and Sluggo begin their rebel yankee yell from the bar
and Brenda Starr throwing her hair to the side
shouts for the waitress who's
out there tossing forks on metal trays
as trumpeter hits his high note
and Jazz Fan says shut up to
noisy Lois Pain In The Ass who smirks
and cuddles up with Lothar as he sips cognac &
rubs Mandrake's thigh while
thief Robin Hood and Maid Marian play leg and lip games in front of
Topsy and Dragon Lady rolling their eyes while
tourists pat feet anywhere
but on the beat
and it goes like that
whenever the music starts
they start

DEADLY RADIATION BLUES

I've seen rubble left by earthquakes
seen erupting volcanoes & devastating avalanches too
I've seen typhoons rising from oceans
seen tornadoes ripping hurricanes howling
and forest fires out of control
Now a nuclear reactor is exploding
and I've got those Chernobyl Three Mile Island Blues

I've seen flash floods & landslides
seen streets turned into red rivers roaring
I've seen thunderbolts & cyclones
and seen blizzards & sandstorms blasting & blowing
Now a nuclear reactor is exploding
and I've got those Chernobyl Three Mile Island Blues

I've seen reservoirs dry up
and knew that moisture in the soil could cease to exist
I've seen objects destroyed by lightning
seen humans stripped of flesh trees stripped of leaves
bones stripped of bones in a drought
Now the rain showers are coming with radiation
and I've got those Chernobyl Three Mile Island Blues

I've seen photos of Nagasaki & Hiroshima
I've heard cries swirling from a chemical plant in Bhopal India
I've seen radioactive dust in Nevada & Utah
Heard screams echoing in from the Ural Mountains too
Now a nuclear reactor is exploding
and I've got those Chernobyl Three Mile Island Blues

I've thrown away milk & lettuce
washed my hair my hands & my shoes
but the winds keep shifting & drifting
and I've got those Chernobyl Three Mile Island Blues

Reactors breed plutonium
blood cells pay their dues

radiation keeps leaking & seeping
and I've got the Chernobyl Three Mile Island Blues

Nuclear power plants can't be dismantled
no way to dispose of the waste
we've got to shut down those reactors
or have the Chernobyl Three Mile Island Blues

Deadly radiation levels high
deadly radiation flying in the sky
deadly radiation swarming with debris
deadly radiation dropping in the sea
deadly radiation forming other clouds
deadly radiation steaming in the bowels
deadly radiation falling through and through
and I've got the Chernobyl Three Mile Island Deadly Radiation Blues

NEW YORK NEW YORK

New York New York
you old sentimental pothole in the head
posing like a tall unemployed parking meter
with two shower caps on
you old subway step of chewed apples and used condoms
resting in front of the lucky spot chop bar
you old sweat-suit wearing sweetpea streaked with
blood from everywhere
you old high-rising rump of pigeon poop on
roof of the Lover Boy Barber Shop
you are
still militaristically coded
still slave-tradish and bullish
still inflated fixated and ready to
jack up your greed in greed of
an executive order
that's you
fine-tuning your capitalistic cock
on four o'clock dot of carnivorous fangs
you big old filthy fetish doll sitting on
hood of a white graffitied truck
smelling like a funky paper mill from Ashdown Arkansas
I see you
trying to remember your immense self-conscious self at
the Remember Me Beauty Parlor
that's you
pants down on butt
bumpersticker on nose
snow-covered garbage-heap belly stuffed in
a black leather jacket

BLUES BOP FOR DIZ

In the bebop band at Minton's
there was a very beautiful trumpet player
who could walk the cliffs at dawn like a Dogon
put dry clay on mouth of a slow blues
groove high
& oop bop sha bam
a kooka mop
in the hot house of Minton's

A very beautiful-sounding trumpet player
with so much confrontational stress
so much cheek inflatiation
so much accelerating concentration
so much chromaticizing in the pistons
of the oo blah dee at Minton's

A very beautiful trumpet player
with such a torrential outburst of spitballs
such forceful streams of aerophonic breath
such mysterious piercing winds
such an array of terrifying cuts on
drum cans of Manteca Manteca
in the rough house at Minton's at Monroe's
a very beautiful trumpet player carrying
sharp pitches of the path
from Gorée to South Carolina & back with
salt peanuts in Akan of Cubano Bop
in ashé of Tin Tin Deo
oo papa odobo   salt peanuts   salt peanuts
in the hot house at Minton's at Monroe's
a very beautiful sounding trumpet player
who could intensify & energize & dynamize the changes
in cool breeze of the caravan
who could pop up & have more punch
in overall tone of the reference
who could transpose clowning

into another composition of contrasting sounds
who could elaborate & agitate & illuminate the voltage
in Tunisia
& oo bop sha bam
down round midnight
groovin high and bopping the blues
in the bebop band at Minton's at Monroe's
A very beautiful trumpet player

LEAVE THAT SONG ALONE

Leave that song alone
it has already been sung
by the one with divination basket in throat
by singer with competitive scrapers in lungs
by the double-gong mouth singers of satire
by the singer with marimba-sounding sound box
the one with Chokwe dialect in up-tempo conversations
the singer with calabash resonator cheeks
the one singing through teeth arranged like xylophone keys
the staccato clicking singers in Bakongo hairdos
the signifying high-frequency singer in harmolodic mode
the one with impeccable announcements coming through the ribcage
      Leave that song alone
      It has already been sung by
the husky-voice singer with emotional overtones in the nose
the one holding different ranges of time in nasal passageways
the singer with phonatious flow of noontime shrills in the air
the one at home in a nest of trombones
the sarcastic singer with microphone in diaphragm
the one with fine & melancholy breathing activity
the singer with vibrato of bees buzzing between lips
the one whose vocal habits are out of sync with structure of the tune
the singer with a complex of signaling devices in the chewing muscle
the one sounding like a crying jackal
      Leave that song alone
      It has already been sung by
the singer with strong wind in the windpipe
the one with deep-rooted solitude in the bronchial tube
the off-key dissonance singers
the one with four-octave range in
orange juice vodka serenade of the sunset limited
the singer with siren-calling jaws
the one with the baby-talking tongue tip
the singer yodeling out in all registers
the one with pineywoods-smelling breath stream
the singer specializing in spatial relationships

the one with a foxhole of sparrows in the vocal folds
the invincible singers with pretty tonality of tones singing
    Leave that song alone
    It has already been sung   sang sing & sung

WHAT'S YOUR TAKE

If a two-headed goat pisses its
long piss of death for your
conversion into a free trade zone
If napalm is being buried in the ground
between tuner of concert pianos and
the pioneer of mathematical analysis
If the corporate terminology settles in
        your mouth like a sweat shop
If a hyena shows you how to eat yourself up
& the blowflies blow your way
& you become like shredded flesh on
      teeth of the IMF
      Watch out
You are in the globalization economic domination process
      Now what's your take
If the world's most potent drink comes from
juice of a festering sore called
      institutionalized brutality
If the most extravagant treaty of abuse
sits like an occupying force on
broken body of an abandoned child
& if the political strategy is to be
      both covert and overt
at the same time on the same level
& if intimidation becomes a patriotic
      theme song called Intimidation
& responsibility remains a potty-training session
for all those holding their tee tees & wee wees
& if a newborn baby comes out looking like
      2 pounds of soggy grape
after a nuclear reactor meltdown
& if you find yourself radioactively depleted
invaded bombed out borderless dislocated delinked
      Watch out
You're in the globalization domination process
      Now what's your take

112

KEYS TO THE CITY

Fascinating compelling
        deep rooted
in the mainstay of avalanche boots
                visceral mixes
the peacock spreading wings
          in memory of
poetry laughing to keep from crying
   & world bank trying to keep from laughing
all right   okay
             get out of here
with your
cupcake   brillo pad vampire-monkey-hairdo self
        great
       amazing
     compliments of the house
     one night stand
            jazz history
         sophisticated frogs
       hammerhead sharks
this is a great SM58 microphone day
in the taste of the smell of the fix of obscurity
        so many lyrics to
         write on broken guitars
so much electricity
to eat up
   and erupt into Lightnin' Hopkins
double time
half time
time of instinctive action
            out front
   in all stability
& multidimensional thinking
       a big asphalt storm
the road
restless
  obsessive

ride you like a horse
into Tutuola's jungle
                turn you loose
& let you say why
        the French colonial empire fell
at Dien Bien Phu
        how apartheid came apart
at Cuito Cuanavale
        and furthermore
I have the trail
        I'm in the territory
I don't need the three stooges of jazz criticism
                to tell me anything
Frank Lowe has keys to the city of Memphis
        play out
                play in
close the door
        open the line
harmolodicize & harmonize
        in the harmattan
                of your head

THE MAMBO LESSON

Yesterday took off its shoes
and became an unpopular song
today will end like a stunned fish in
tomorrow's unequal distribution of
emptiness
as the sun makes its entrance
without public support into
the clairvoyance of your
unsweetened panty hose
& I am already
smoking an image
that will bite me
before I change my tongue
so don't forget your skull
your fossil fuel
your utopian teeth